AF679500

ALTERED AUDIO

Podcasting Demystified

Clear Advice, Real Tools, and Zero Gatekeeping

by Steve Phillips

Published by

GeekCast Radio Network, LLC

First Edition

Copyright Page Information

Altered Audio: Podcasting Demystified *Clear Advice, Real Tools, and Zero Gatekeeping*

© 2025 by Steve Phillips All rights reserved.

No part of this publication may be reproduced, stored in a retrieval system, or transmitted in any form or by any means—electronic, mechanical, photocopying, recording, or otherwise—without prior written permission from the author, except for brief quotations used in reviews or academic discussion as permitted by copyright law.

This work is registered with the United States Copyright Office.

ISBN: 979-8-3495-0459-4 First Edition, August 2025

Published by GeekCast Radio Network, LLC Self-published via Kindle Direct Publishing

Written by Steve Phillips Edited by Steve Phillips Interior Layout by Microsoft Copilot (AI Assistance) Cover Design by Steve Phillips

Author Website: https://StevenCPhillips.net

GeekCast Radio Network Website: https://geekcastradio.com

Disclaimer: This book is intended as a resource for individuals interested in starting a podcast. It provides general guidance, tools, and insights for both aspiring and experienced podcasters. The author and publisher make no guarantees regarding outcomes, accuracy, or the suitability of the content for specific situations. Readers are encouraged to perform their own research and consult professional advisors when necessary.

Table of Contents

How to Use This Book

Visual Layout Prompts

Icon	Meaning	Usage Tip
💡	**Pro Tip**	Use for time-saving tricks and advice nuggets
🔧	**Technical Insight**	Place next to gear, workflow, or tool suggestions
🎙️	**Voice-Forward Advice**	Denote personal experience or hosting insight
🧠	**Reflective Prompt**	Cue introspective questions or journaling exercises

Prologue: How a $9 Mic Changed Everything

I started podcasting completely by accident.

My real dream? Becoming a voice actor. In 2005, that dream led me to buy my first mic—a $9 Labtec desk mic that sounded like it came free with a cereal box. Still, it launched me into the world of fan dubs. I was voicing Transformers characters in Japanese series like *Headmasters*, experimenting with editing, and learning by trial, error, and a whole lot of re-recording. Then I bought a USB headset with a microphone built-in for somewhat better audio quality.

By 2006, I started listening to shows like *TFwire* and *This Week in Geek*—and funny enough, I've worked with both in the years since. When *TFwire* opened up auditions for *War Stories: A Transformers Fan Fiction Podcast*, I jumped in. Fifteen episodes later, I was narrating and voice acting my way through audiobook-style productions that ignited my passion for longform storytelling.

In 2007, I guest-starred on *TFwire's* main show to dissect the first *Transformers* live-action film. Shortly after that, I appeared on their gaming show *PlayOn!*—pretty sure we were talking about *Super Smash Bros. Brawl*. That chat led me to pitch my own movie review podcast—*Weekend at the Movies*—which later evolved into *Movie Week in REview*.

And in August 2008, I launched my first original show: *All Things Transformers*. That was the turning point. The mic had gotten better, but I still had a lot to learn.

Building the GeekCast Radio Network

In 2009, Michael "TFG1Mike" Blanchard and I founded the GeekCast Radio Network—a place where we could pull all our podcast ideas under one roof. What started with Transformers talk quickly grew into a full-fledged network: *ToonCast*, *MWIRE*, *ToyCast*, *GeekCast Radio*, *The Tele-Cast*, and more.

2010 was a game-changer. We became the first network to cover *Beast Wars* and *Beast Machines* in their entirety with *The Beast Unleashed Podcast*. That deep dive into niche fandoms became part of our DNA.

In 2011, we pulled off one of our most ambitious feats: the *Top 100 Animated Series of All Time* countdown. We partnered with geek sites to create a definitive list that sparked debate, passion, and a whole lot of feedback. *(Let's just say we weren't shy about doing better than IGN.)* That format would later be carried over into a Transformers-specific version years later among over half a dozen other countdowns.

By 2013, shows like *The Pull Bag* and *Altered Geek* gave the network a new voice—one that blended commentary, pop culture, and the shifting media landscape through my lens as a creator and lifelong geek.

Through the 2010s, we passed milestone after milestone: 300+ episodes on flagship shows, over 1,000-episode credits for some hosts, and events like GCRN WarZ. In 2019, we celebrated 10 years with a site redesign and the start of our video content era.

And in 2024—our 15th anniversary—I overhauled the site again to focus on our strengths: podcasting, gaming videos, and deep-dive interviews. With 40 shows and 10–20 rotating contributors, we're still obsessed with pop culture, animation, comic books, and, naturally, *Transformers*.

Teaching the Next Generation

When I moved from Michigan to Colorado, I brought the network with me—but I also brought a new perspective. Balancing GCRN with a full-time job and raising a family *(two kids keep things lively)*, I found time for something I'd never tried before: teaching.

In June 2024, I led a podcasting workshop at the Boys & Girls Club of Larimer County. A little over a dozen 10-year-olds lit up as we talked about mics, storytelling, voice acting, interviews conducted and how to bring their voices into the world. Some interviewed me on the spot; others asked for voice impressions. It was electric.

That day reminded me why I started: not for numbers or metrics, but for connection. Podcasting gave me confidence, creativity, and a sense of voice—and I realized it was time to help someone else find theirs.

Introduction: A Rebellion in Progress

(And You're Invited)

So, you want to start a podcast.

That sentence might sound simple—but in 2025, it's practically a battle cry. Because today, content is *everywhere*. Podcasts are *everywhere*. Creators are hustling, grinding, chasing algorithms and sponsorships that ask them to tweak, tone down, or trade in their voice for something "more marketable."

This book is the opposite of that.

Altered Audio is for the curious, the nostalgic, the niche-obsessed, the introverts with something to say, and the fans who never saw their fandoms reflected in mainstream media—until they hit "record" themselves. It's for the brave souls launching shows from closets, basements, spare rooms, garages, or their car *(Just not while in motion)*. It's for those who still believe podcasting can be personal, portable, and powerful.

I've recorded over 4,000 episodes. I've co-founded a podcast network built on geek passion and grassroots grit. I've seen it all: the rise of audio drama, the fall of Stitcher, the flood of video pods and AI noise. Through it all, one truth remains:

> *Independent podcasting isn't dying. It's evolving. And it's never mattered more.*

This book won't sell you a "10k downloads in 10 days" gimmick. It won't tell you to become a YouTube-first, subscription-walled content machine. What it *will* do is show you how to:

- Launch with confidence and intention—even if all you have is a USB mic and a head full of ideas
- Stay grounded in your voice, your values, and your audience—even as trends shift and burnout knocks
- Learn from 20 years of trial and error: the wins, the faceplants, and the quiet moments that mattered most

Inside, we'll talk about gear (without gatekeeping), promotion (without pandering), growth (without grift), monetization (without losing your soul), and the subtle art of showing up with authenticity *every single week*.

Because here's the truth most books skip:

> *You're not just starting a show. You're starting a connection. One listener at a time.*

Whether you're creating your first episode or questioning your 400th, *Altered Audio* is here to remind you why this medium still feels like magic—and how to protect that magic while building something real, resonant, and deeply yours.

So pull up the mic, creator.

We've got stories to tell—and this time, *you* lead the narrative.

Chapter 1: The Myth of the "Right Way"

There's a myth that still lingers in every new podcaster's mind: that there's a *right* way to do this. A formula. A blueprint. A master guide written by audio sages with golden microphones.

Spoiler: there's not.

What *does* exist is a messy, powerful medium still being shaped by creators recording from closets, bunkers, bedrooms, and burnout. Voices that stumble, laugh, learn—and show up because they have something to say. Not because someone told them they could.

When I started, I didn't know what "levels" were. I didn't know the "best" hosting platform. All I knew was I had a perspective, a pop culture itch, and a head full of knowledge no one else was telling in my corner of the internet. That was enough.

This chapter isn't about how to be perfect—it's about how to begin *anyway*. We'll cover what you really need to get started (spoiler: it's not much).

Whether you're launching your first episode or battling your tenth identity crisis at episode 400, the truth still holds:

Podcasting was never about perfection. It's always been about permission—the kind you give yourself.

Interlude: What Is a Podcast?

Before we dive deeper, let's break it down for the uninitiated (or the overwhelmed).

A podcast is...

- A series of spoken episodes
- Like radio shows, but on-demand
- Available for free on streaming platforms
- A space for *any* topic you can imagine—from deep dives into Norse mythology to unscripted kitchen-table chats discussing the latest films or hobbies

Why people love them:

- Learn new things
- Get entertained
- Discover niche passions
- Listen while walking, cleaning, or commuting

In other words, podcasts are flexible, personal, and powerful. They're built for multitasking brains and curiosity chasers.

The Real Starter Pack: What You Actually Need to Begin

Forget the shopping carts full of gear. You don't need a fancy mic, a million-dollar studio, or a team of editors to start a podcast. You need three things:

- A voice that wants to be heard
- A reason to speak
- And the guts to hit record

That's it. Really.

If we're being generous, here's the full starter kit:

- **A decent mic** — USB is just fine. My first? A $9 Labtec desk mic that probably came bundled with a cereal box prize *(I kid, but you get the picture)*. It was terrible. But it got me started.
- **A pair of analog headphones** — To keep your audio from echoing like you're in a cave.
- **Free editing software** — Audacity, GarageBand, or even your phone.
- **Somewhere quiet-ish** — Closets *(filled rooms)* > cathedrals *(open spaces)*, when it comes to echo control.
- **An idea that makes your inner geek light up** — Trust me, that passion will carry you further than any mixer board ever could.

What you *don't* need: A logo on Day One. A website. A monetization plan. A viral clip strategy. That can all come later. Right now, it's just you, your story, and the space you're about to create.

The Mental Gremlins: What Really Stops You

Let's be real—It's rarely the gear. It's the gremlins.

The ones that whisper in your head just before you hit "record." The ones that hijack your confidence before Episode One is even outlined.

Let's name them. Let's reframe them. Let's take away their power.

- **Gremlin #1: "What if no one listens?"** Great. That's your creative sandbox. No pressure. No expectations. Only freedom to play, test, explore—and discover your real voice.
- **Gremlin #2: "I'll sound awkward."** Yep. You will. Every creator does. But talking into a mic is a muscle—and the only way to build it... is to use it.
- **Gremlin #3: "Someone's already doing this."** Maybe. But they're not doing it *your way*. Your lived experience, your tone, your fandom mashups—they're the unrepeatable part.
- **Gremlin #4: "I don't sound professional."** Here's a secret: listeners crave *real* more than *radio*. And authenticity? That's louder than perfection every time.
- **Gremlin #5: "I'm not ready yet."** Nobody is. You get ready by starting—not the other way around.

So here's your job: Talk back. Not with arrogance. Not with ego. With truth. With joy. With your own geek-fired voice. Just be authentic.

Those mental gremlins aren't roadblocks. They're signs that you care. Keep going anyway.

Redefining Success (Hint: It's Not in the Charts)

Once upon a podcast, "success" meant connection. Then the algorithm showed up.

Suddenly, creators were chasing downloads, clips, charts, sponsorships—metrics dressed up as meaning. And hey, stats *can* be useful. But if you start measuring your worth in numbers, burnout moves in fast.

Let's redefine it.

Success isn't a rank or even a race. It's a moment.

Did you show up even when your confidence wobbled? Did someone message you and say, "That episode hit me right in the gut"? Did you finally hit "publish" after five false starts?

That's success. That's resonance.

Here's mine: When *All Things Transformers* launched, there were no vanity metrics. No pressure. Just geeky passion and the thrill of knowing someone—maybe just one person—was nodding along on the other side of the feed.

Success wasn't about being #1. It was about making *one* person feel seen.

So here's your version—build it yourself.

- Maybe it's finishing your first season.

- Maybe it's recording without second-guessing every line.
- Maybe it's giving someone a reason to laugh during a hard week.

Forget the charts. Track what actually matters. Impact > impressions. Every single time.

Your First Step: Start Ugly, Start Real

Now that we've dropped the myths and reset the stakes, it's time for action.

Your mission, should you choose to accept it: Record a 2-minute message to your future self. Say why you want to start this show. Say what you hope it becomes. No script. No edits. Just your voice, raw and real.

Don't share it yet. Just listen to it later—after 10 episodes, 100 episodes, or whenever you're questioning if this was worth it. Let that moment be your compass.

Because here's the secret: **podcasting isn't about having all the answers—it's about having the courage to start anyway.**

And you, creator? You've got what it takes.

Chapter 1: Quick Recap — Start Ugly, Start Real

💭 Reflect

- What myths have you absorbed about how podcasting "should" work?
- Which gremlin whispers to you most—and what would you say back if the mic were live?

🎙️ Build

- Record a two-minute message to your future self: no script, no polish—just purpose.
- Write a single sentence that defines your creative spark. Doesn't have to be perfect. Just has to be honest.

🔧 Refine

- Toss the idea of download numbers as your North Star. What does *your* success actually look like?
- Make a checklist for your first recording setup—barebones, functional, and ready to move.

Chapter 2: The Soul of Audio

In a world obsessed with visuals, why does audio still matter?

Because listening is intimate. It's personal. It's the only medium where your voice—raw and unfiltered—can sit in someone's ear while they drive, cook, walk their dog, or unwind from the day. Audio doesn't demand attention—it *invites* it. It doesn't interrupt your life—it *joins* it. And in a culture addicted to screens, that makes it quietly revolutionary.

When I first picked up the mic in 2006, I wasn't thinking about intimacy. I was thinking about fandoms. About storytelling. About how cool it was to create something from scratch. But over time, I realized something deeper: the magic of audio isn't just in the message. It's in the *feeling* it creates.

The Power of Voice

Your voice is more than sound—it's signature. Identity. Humanity.

People can hear if you're smiling. They can feel hesitation. They can sense joy, fatigue, sarcasm, and sincerity. Voice communicates what text can't and what video tries too hard to simulate. That's why podcasting hits different—it connects at the gut level.

Why Audio-First Still Wins (Even in 2025)

Sure, TikToks are trending. YouTube shorts are algorithm gold. But here's what those can't replicate:

- **Focus** — Audio lets your listener sink in, without pop-ups, notifications, or autoplay chaos. It's long-form presence in a short-form world.
- **Flexibility** — Your audience can tune in anywhere. No screen needed. Hands-free, eyes-free, always accessible.
- **Freedom** — No ring light. No fancy camera. No gimmicks. Just your voice and a message that matters. That's creative liberation.

Being audio-first isn't outdated—it's *timeless*. And in today's noisy content arena, it just might be your edge.

Listening As A Superpower

Here's something I've learned after nearly 20 years behind the mic: the best podcasters aren't just talkers. They're *listeners*.

Listening reveals what your audience really cares about. It sharpens your story. Refines your tone. Guides your growth. Before you speak *to* your community, you've got to listen *with* them.

So the next time you prep a show, don't just hit record. Hit **pause**. Listen to:

- Your favorite shows
- The subtext in your reviews

- The silence between your words
- And most of all—your *why*

Because the soul of audio? It isn't tech. It isn't trends. It's *connection*.

And that starts with *you*.

Chapter 2: Quick Recap — The Soul Beneath the Sound

💭 Reflect

- How does your voice carry emotion, even when unscripted?
- What does audio allow you to share that video or text cannot?

🎙️ Build

- Listen to your favorite podcast and identify what makes the host feel authentic.
- Try recording with two tone styles—reflective vs. excited—and play them back.

🔧 Refine

- Write down three words that describe the emotional energy you want in your episodes.
- Outline your listening rituals—what can you learn from how *you* consume audio?

Chapter 3: Formats, Storytelling, and the Power of Content

Not every podcast needs to sound the same—and that's the beauty of it. Podcasting gives you the freedom to define your show's personality, structure, and impact. Whether you're flying solo or guiding a full production team, it all begins with format and flows into storytelling.

Understanding Podcast Formats

Here's a menu of formats to choose from—or combine. The right one will complement your style and elevate your message:

Format	What It Brings
Solo Commentary	A direct line from your brain to your audience's ears—personal, reflective, opinionated.
Interview	Fresh perspectives from guests. Excellent for learning, storytelling, and audience discovery.
Panel Discussions	Roundtable energy. Multiple voices and viewpoints encourage dynamic engagement.
Conversational/Co-Hosted	Think witty banter, shared stories, and friendship at the mic—relatable and real.
Narrative Storytelling	Carefully crafted arcs, often with sound design—like audio documentaries or exposés.
Fictional/Audio Drama	Scripted tales with immersive sound. Think old-school radio reimagined.
Educational	Dive deep into a subject to teach and inform. Break down complex ideas for curious minds.

Format	What It Brings
News & Current Events	Timely takes on the world. From daily digests to deep-dive explainers.
Themed/Topic-Specific	Geek out on your niche—pop culture, tech, retro toys, paranormal mysteries—you name it.
Hybrid	Mix formats across episodes—or even within a single episode—for creative variety.

💡 ***Pro Tip:*** *Your format isn't set in stone. Evolve as your show evolves. Start simple, and experiment over time.*

Content Is King

Content isn't just what you say—it's how you say it, why it matters, and how it connects.

This chapter is about turning your format into *something that resonates*. From the first word to the final beat, content is your chance to create meaning—and build loyalty.

The Anatomy of a Great Episode

Every episode is a story. Whether it's an interview, a solo rant, or a deep dive into a niche topic, the best episodes follow a structure that keeps listeners engaged.

🎬 Act 1: The Hook

Start strong. Your opening sets the tone and stakes. Ask a question, share a surprising fact, or tease the journey ahead.

🎭 Act 2: The Core

This is the meat of your episode—the insights, stories, or conversations that deliver on your promise. Keep it focused, but don't be afraid to let your personality shine.

🎤 **Act 3: The Close**

End with impact. Recap the key takeaways, invite listener action (subscribe, share, comment), and leave them wanting more.

Hosting an Interview: Preparation, Presence, and Professionalism

Interviewing isn't just conversation—it's connection. The best interviews come from planning, intention, and the respect you show your guest.

Before the Mic Turns On

- Research their background and latest work
- Send an info packet with your format, audience, and sample questions
- Clarify tech setup and expectations: audio quality matters

During the Interview

- Start with a warm welcome
- Listen actively, and let them finish their thoughts
- Ask thoughtful follow-ups—react and riff naturally
- Keep the energy collaborative, not performative

After the Interview

- Send a thank-you note
- Share the episode, tagged and promoted
- Leave the door open for future collaboration

When you host well, your guests shine—and your audience feels the difference.

Finding Your Tone

Your tone is your show's personality. It's how you connect with your audience. Are you casual and conversational? Formal and polished? Geeky and niche?

Try a few test recordings. Listen back. The tone that feels most like *you* is usually the one listeners will respond to most.

Building Listener Loyalty

Great content doesn't just earn downloads—it earns *trust*. Here's how to build a loyal audience:

- **Consistency** — Show up on schedule. It builds habit and expectation.
- **Engagement** — Respond to emails, DMs, comments. Make it a conversation.
- **Authenticity** — Be real. Be imperfect. Your honesty is your magnet.
- **Value** — Teach something. Make them laugh. Make them feel. Leave them better than you found them.

Closeout: Your Content, Your Connection

The format is the frame. The story is the engine. But content—that's the heart of your podcast. So what's your voice? What's the experience you want to create?

You've got a mic and a message. Let's turn it into a movement.

Chapter 3: Quick Recap — Formats, Flow, and Storytelling

Reflect

- What kind of format excites you most: solo, interview, hybrid?
- What's one story you've always wanted to tell on-mic?

Build

- Create a draft episode outline using the "Hook–Core–Close" structure.
- Choose a format and record a 5-minute sample. Listen for tone and pacing.

Refine

- Review your hosting style—do you listen actively or talk through pauses?
- Set a goal: one new content style to experiment with over the next 3 episodes.

Chapter 4: Mic Check — Welcome to the Stage

Let's drop the myth now: great audio doesn't require a studio, a sponsor, or a soft-focus YouTube setup. You don't need a trust fund to start talking—you just need a quiet room, a mic, and something to say.

Podcasting shouldn't feel gated. It should feel possible. Whether you're just thinking about your first episode or already a few in, this chapter is your no-fluff, real-world sound guide for making audio that connects.

Your Voice, Amplified

Great gear doesn't create great content—you do. But the right mic and a little know-how can make your message land with more power and less hiss.

I started with a $9 mic that sounded like it was haunted by dial-up demons. That setup taught me to problem-solve, edit like a maniac, and chase clarity without chasing perfection. That learning curve? Worth every earbud.

Audio Setup Tiers: From Scrappy to Studio

Tier	Gear	Notes
🟢 **Start Mode**	USB mics (Blue Yeti, Mackie EM-USB, Samson Q2U, ATR2100)	Plug-and-play ease; add pop filter & foam windscreen
🟡 **Evolve Mode**	XLR mics (Rode PodMic, Shure MV7) + Interface (Focusrite Scarlett 2i2)	Cleaner signal, more control, more to tweak

🔴 Pro Mode	Shure SM7B, Electro-Voice RE20 + MixPre-3 or Rodecaster Pro II	Multitrack, onboard effects, custom room setup

💡 ***Pro Tip:*** No mic will save a boring show. No interface will inject passion. That still has to come from you.

Taming the Room: Soundproofing Without Studio Money

A killer mic in a bad room is like the Enterprise with failing warp drive. Or another analogy, a Corvette on gravel—loud, messy, and not what you paid for. Here's how to clean up your space without burning your budget:

- 🎙️ Record in a closet full of clothes
- 🛏️ Drape a blanket or comforter behind you
- 🛋️ Use pillows and furniture to absorb echo
- 🔇 Silence appliances, close windows, and record during your quietest hours
- 👂 Clap and listen for bounce—then tweak

My own setup? A treated spare room with movable foam panels, closet coats, and furniture arranged to diffuse sound. Clean. Controlled. Adaptable.

Multi-Host, Remote Recording: Your Voice, From Anywhere

Remote recording isn't second-best—it's the reality for most modern creators. Whether you're capturing co-host banter across continents or hosting guests from different time zones, your gear and software need to be sharp, stable, and simple.

The goal is flexibility without sacrificing audio quality—or your sanity.

Remote-Friendly Gear

- **Mics**: Dynamic USBs like Blue Yeti (cardioid mode), Rode PodMic, ATR2100, Shure MV7
- **Interfaces**: Focusrite Scarlett 2i2, Zoom PodTrak P4 (or skip for USB simplicity)
- **Monitoring**: Wired headphones only—Audio-Technica ATH-M50x, Mackie MC-350
- **Accessories**: Pop filter, windscreen, shock mount (matched to your mic, not your mood)

🔧 ***Technical Insight:*** Pop filters are like socks for your mic. They keep the sound warm and soft.

Remote Recording Platforms

Platform	Strengths	Considerations
Zoom	Familiar, local recording, decent quality	Enable separate audio track recording
Discord + CRAIG/GIARC Bot	Multitrack files (FLAC/WAV), easy download	Needs prep and sync, but modular
Zencastr	Studio sound, browser-based	Requires solid internet
SquadCast	Video + separate tracks	Paid tier for full features
Cleanfeed	Real-time browser mix	Best for tech-savvy creators
Riverside.fm	Local audio, pro quality	Higher pricing, great polish

🔧 ***Technical Insight:*** Always do a test run before the real deal. Remote doesn't mean reckless.

Recording & Editing: Not a Chore, a Craft

You've got your raw audio—now it's time to shape it without sanding off the soul.

Core Editing Moves

- Trim long pauses and dead air
- Cut filler words (or leave them if they're part of your charm)
- Level speaker volumes for balance
- Adjust pacing so the convo feels tight but natural

Audio Tools Worth Knowing

Tool	Price	Use Case
Descript	Freemium	Text-based edits, fast cleanup
Audacity	Free	Multitrack DIY editing
Adobe Audition	$22.99/mo	Advanced effects, production flow
Auphonic / Adobe Speech Enhance	Freemium	Auto cleanup, voice polish

🔧 ***Technical Insight:*** You don't need to be an audio engineer. You just need to care enough to make it clear.

Repeatable = Sustainable

Over 4,000 episodes later, here's what keeps me sane:

- 🎧 **DAW Templates:** Save recurring track layouts and effects

- 📄 **Episode Docs:** Notes, promos, and calls to action prepped in advance
- 🧘 **Let It Go**: 90% done beats 100% perfect—every time

Bonus Wisdom They Don't Print on Mic Boxes

- 🔧 A condenser picks up everything. A dynamic picks up mostly *you*.
- 🔧 Cardioid pattern = sounds great up front, meh behind
- 🔧 Record separate tracks for every speaker if you can—your editor (you?) will thank you
- ❌ Don't eat on the mic. Or eat the mic. Seriously.
- 🕒 Your episode can be any length—as long as it's intentional

Closeout: Make the Mic Yours

The gear evolves. Your confidence grows. But your voice? That's always been the point.

My best episodes weren't the ones with perfect sound. They were the ones where I showed up—prepared, imperfect, but fully in.

So... mics on. What do you want to say?

Chapter 4: Quick Recap — Make the Mic Yours

💭 Reflect

- Is your current setup helping or hindering your voice?
- What do you need more: gear upgrades or space treatment?

🎙 Build

- Record and test your current setup—what sounds off, what sounds solid?
- Make a checklist for audio treatment in your space (even blankets count).

🔧 Refine

- Research one new mic or recording tool that aligns with your goals.
- Define your sweet spot: a setup that works for both your voice and your workflow.

Chapter 5: Behind the Waveform

Editing as Emotion, Structure, and Voice

You've got a voice. You've got the setup. You've even got episodes in the wild. Now comes the part most creators dread—and where most of the magic actually happens: post-production.

But editing isn't just about cleanup. It's where your ideas sharpen, your pacing finds rhythm, and your message gets space to breathe.

This chapter isn't a tutorial. It's a mindset shift.

Editing as Storytelling

What you cut and what you keep? That's the soul of your show. Editing shapes tone, energy, and emotion just as much as your mic does.

- **Remove distractions**: But leave texture. That nervous laugh might *be* the moment.
- **Respect silence**: Breathing room creates gravity.
- **Trust your instinct**: If it drags, tighten it. If it hits, protect it.

Tools That Fit (Not Frustrate)

You don't need every knob and slider. You need gear that fits *you*.

Adobe Audition (Your Daily Driver)

- Multitrack editing, precise noise reduction, non-destructive effects
- Podcast presets, Essential Sounds, and track templates
- My hub for over 4,000 episodes—because it bends to my workflow

Descript

- Word-based editing + auto transcription
- Great for scripting, first-pass edits, and fast cleanups

Audacity

- Free, reliable, open-source
- Perfect for beginners or fast, dirty fixes

GarageBand (Mac Only)

- Built-in, intuitive interface
- Limited flexibility—but powerful for solo hosts

Bonus Tools

Tool	Use Case
Auphonic	Loudness leveling, auto cleanup
Reaper	Pro-grade, affordable, deep learning curve
Hindenburg	Designed for storytellers and journalists

Picking Your Ideal DAW

Goal	Best DAW(s)	Why
Just starting	Audacity, GarageBand	Free, simple, forgiving
Speed + simplicity	Descript	Edits like a document, AI-supported
Pro audio production	Adobe Audition	Complete control, endless customization
Affordable powerhouse	Reaper	Cheap, complex, customizable
Story-driven dialogue	Hindenburg	Tailored for voice-centric work

🎙 ***Voice-Forward Advice:*** Start with what feels manageable. Then build toward what feels like *you*.

Quick Glossary: Audio Tools Worth Knowing

- **DAW (Digital Audio Workstation):** Software used to record, edit, and mix audio. Examples include Audacity, Adobe Audition, Reaper.
- **Audio Hijack:** Mac-based software that captures audio from apps, inputs, and system sources—great for multitrack recording remotely.
- **Normalization:** Balancing volume levels across tracks or episodes for consistency.

- **Compression:** A tool that softens loud peaks and lifts quiet moments to make your mix smoother.
- **EQ (Equalization):** Adjusts frequency balance (bass, mids, treble) to enhance clarity.
- **Separate Tracks:** Recording individual audio streams for each speaker—vital for remote hosts or interviews and clean edits.

💡 ***Pro Tip:*** You don't need to master everything overnight—but learning the language sharpens your instincts.

Multitrack Like a Pro

Multitrack is your control room—where creative chaos becomes clarity.

Why It Matters:

- **Precision editing**: Fix one voice without affecting the other
- **Creative layering**: Add music, SFX, ambiance without crowding speech
- **Consistent sound**: Apply effects only where they're needed

Setup Tips:

- Record with multiple inputs using interfaces like Focusrite Scarlett 2i2
- Build labeled DAW templates (Host, Guest, Music, FX)

- Always test before recording: levels, space, interference

My Workflow:

- Import into Audition using custom track layouts
- Clean audio using built-in noise reduction tools
- Balance voices individually
- Apply light EQ, compression, maybe a touch of reverb
- Mix, listen, tweak—until the story sounds like you

🎙️ ***Voice-Forward Advice:*** My presets are tuned to hit between -9dB and -3dB. Just enough headroom, always clean.

Pre-Edit Checklist

Before you ever trim a second:

- ✅ Mic placement: 5-8 inches from your mouth
- ✅ Quiet room: Eliminate fans, fridges, background chatter, washer/dryer, 3D printer, etc.
- ✅ Consistent environment: Repeatable sound is polished sound
- ✅ Recording levels: Monitor in real-time to avoid clipping or dropouts

Start strong. Finish smooth.

AI Without Losing the Human

AI tools can lighten the load—but don't let them flatten your soul.

Tools That Help:

- **Adobe Speech Enhance**: Cleans low-quality audio
- **Descript Cleanup**: Removes filler words & silences
- **Auphonic**: Balances levels across tracks
- **Chat-based planning tools**: Brainstorm structure, not voice

Where It Shines:

- Batch leveling
- First-pass cleanup
- Episode scaffolding

Where It Doesn't:

- Emotional nuance
- Over-editing risk
- Tone distortion

Your voice isn't just info—it's interpretation.
Use the bots as assistants, not narrators.

The Sacred Delete Key

Editing is compassion.

Every cut directs the listener's attention—and respects their time. You're not removing *you*. You're clarifying *you*.

- 🧠 Ego Check: The cut is not a critique
- 🎯 Purpose First: Keep what earns its place
- 🧹 Silence the clutter: Hiss, hum, tangents? Lose 'em
- 🎙️ Shape the experience: Every edit is a decision in tone

Acoustic Treatment & Sound Barriers

These lived better here in the flow—your guide to keeping the edit as clean as the capture.

- 🧥 Record in closet spaces or thick-curtain corners
- 🎛️ Use acoustic foam, panels, furniture, and carpet to reduce bounce
- 🎙️ Mic accessories matter: shock mounts, filters, furry wind covers
- 📐 Your mic should hear *you,* not your room

Final Fadeout

The best episodes I've ever produced weren't perfect. They were intentional. They were honest. They were mine.

Editing doesn't erase humanity—it enhances it.

Chapter 5: Quick Recap — Shape the Story in Post

💭 **Reflect**

- Do you see editing as cleanup… or creative enhancement?
- How do your editing choices shape tone and trust?

🎙 **Build**

- Try editing a segment two ways—minimal vs. polished. What changes?
- Create an "Editing Prep Checklist" before your next session.

🔧 **Refine**

- Choose one new DAW feature or shortcut to learn this week.
- Draft your personal editing mantra (e.g. "Cut for clarity, keep for humanity").

Chapter 6: Chronicles of Content Creation

From childhood radio dreams to top-tier podcast interviews, content creation has always been about connection—for you, for the GCRN, and for every listener who finds their place in the conversation.

Pivotal Moments: The Signal Finds Its Voice

GeekCast Radio Network wasn't built with a blueprint—it was sparked by instinct. I had something to say. And podcasting gave me the mic to speak it.

What started with imagined radio shows and playful commentary grew into a dynamic outlet for geek culture, storytelling, and connection. From *All Things Transformers* to *Altered Geek* to *Movie Week in REview*, each show added a new dimension—sometimes planned, often improvisational, always passionate.

And the moments stacked up:

- The Top 100 Animated Series Countdown that lit up the comment sections and sparked debate.
- Interviews with voices that shaped fandom—Kevin Conroy, David Kaye, Tom Bergeron and beyond.
- Milestone episodes, deep-dive retrospectives, and enough audio logs to fill a vault.

Each moment wasn't just an episode. It was a bat signal—proof that resonance always mattered more than reach.

When Burnout Hit

(And Why You Came Back)

The podcast feed quieted. Life got loud. The mic sat still—until listeners spoke up.

"Miss your voice." "Is *All Things Transformers* coming back?" "Your show helped me through a rough patch."

I didn't relaunch for metrics. I did it for connection. For the conversation. And for the creators, listeners, and fellow geeks who kept the signal alive—even in silence.

I came back. Three times. And every return was a reminder: The flame's still there. I just needed the space to find it.

Listener Echoes That Shaped the Journey

This isn't just my legacy. It's theirs, too.

The kid at a workshop who asked for a voice impression. The fan who binge-listened 100 episodes and said, "You made my week better." The listener who listened to my early mistakes—because I chose to share them.

These aren't analytics. They're echoes. The quiet proof that the podcast doesn't stop at the upload. It lives in headphones, commutes, and chaotic Tuesdays when someone needed to feel less alone.

"Legacy isn't what you leave behind—it's what you build along the way."

Who Are You Really Talking To?

Content creation isn't about chasing every click—it's about finding clarity, community, and connection. Understanding your audience helps you build deeper relationships.

The View Illusion

Metric	Video Platforms	Podcast Platforms
Views	Often inflated, non-standardized	Reliable, IAB 2.0 certified
Engagement	*Can* be superficial (likes, comments)	Meaningful (listens, feedback)
Retention	Hard to measure accurately depending on the platform	Clear listener drop-off points
Analytics	Varies by platform	Consistent across platforms

💡 ***Pro Tip:*** By focusing on podcast-centric metrics, creators can foster quality engagement and build trust that lasts.

Content That Sticks

Crafting resonant content means aligning passion, format, and delivery with audience expectations. Here's the creative blueprint:

- **Topic Selection**: Relevance, uniqueness, and genuine enthusiasm.
- **Storytelling Formats**: Mix narrative, educational, and interactive approaches.

- **Publishing Cadence**: Prioritize consistency and quality—adjust based on feedback and analytics.

Podcast Naming & Niche Research

Name It Right: Protect Your Identity

Want to avoid podcast purgatory? Do your homework.

Before you launch:

- Search your show name across Apple Podcasts, Spotify, and Google
- Check domain availability and social media handles
- Make it distinct, searchable, and memorable
- Avoid duplicating trending phrases or generic formats

I've had to chase down creators who copied my podcast titles without looking—it's not fun. Protect your brand, honor originality, and make the name yours.

Show Formats & Evolution

Each GCRN program developed its own rhythm:

- **All Things Transformers**: News, feedback, then deep dives—now with call-to-actions placed early.
- **Altered Geek**: Fluid formatting with listener-first adaptation, news commentary, and topical finish.

- **Movie Week in REview (MWIRE)**: Structure anchored by trailers, highlights, lowlights, discussion, ranking and wrap-up.

Adapting formats based on audience behavior and platform feedback has kept the shows fresh and responsive.

Audience Intimacy Over Audience Size

It's not about reaching *everyone*—it's about reaching *the right ones*.

- **Focused Content**: Tailor your message to specific passions and problems.
- **Higher Engagement**: Invested listeners drive conversation and growth.
- **Sustainable Success**: Nurturing a loyal community outperforms fleeting virality.

Social Media with a Soul

Social media can elevate your podcast, but it's important to use it intentionally:

- **Authentic Engagement**: Share your process, respond thoughtfully, and build dialogue.
- **Boundaries Matter**: Avoid burnout by posting with purpose and pacing.
- **Tools to Help**: Use platforms like Buffer or Canva to streamline and amplify your voice.

"Social media is a tool, not a measure of your worth."

AI: Your Creative Co-Pilot

AI unlocks new ways to connect with listeners and refine your content. Here's how to use it wisely:

Audience & Analytics Strategy

- Episode performance breakdowns
- Title and description optimization
- Topic frequency audits
- Listener behavior insights
- Platform comparisons
- Episode length tuning
- Metric-driven refinements

AI Use as a Tool

1. **Integration**: Support production and engagement workflows
2. **Fresh Ideas**: Generate unique episode concepts
3. **Authenticity First**: Use AI as support, not a substitute
4. **Tailored Content**: Refine based on listener data
5. **Balance Human Touch**: Maintain creative integrity

Longevity & Legacy

True success lies in sustaining creativity and building something that lasts:

- **Evolve & Adapt**: Let your content grow with you.
- **Pace Yourself**: Take breaks, protect your energy.
- **Partner Up**: Collaborate to expand ideas and reach.
- **Define Your Mission**: Anchor your voice in values and impact.

"The seeds of the future lie buried in the past." – The Oracle, Beast Machines Transformers

---

As you reflect on the stories, shows, and sparks that defined GCRN's journey, this chapter becomes more than a guide—it's a living archive of passion, growth, and shared purpose.

Chapter 6: Quick Recap — Chronicle What Counts

💭 Reflect

- What moments built your creative identity—milestones or missteps?
- Are you chasing trends… or shaping legacy in real time?

🎙 Build

- Pinpoint three core listener values that align with your content.
- Write a brand bio in two honest, vivid sentences: what you do and why it matters.

🔧 Refine

- Audit your podcast name for originality, searchability, and soul.
- Set a near-term goal for deeper audience connection—less noise, more intimacy.

Chapter 7: Mic in One Hand, Blueprint in the Other

Monetization is an essential pillar of sustaining your creative journey, but it should never undermine your authenticity or the trust you've built with your audience. Below is a curated list of monetization strategies—each offering distinct ways to support your work while staying true to your brand:

Monetization Strategies

Education & Expertise

- Courses or Workshops
- Coaching or Consulting
- Book Writing

Physical & Digital Products

- Merchandise Sales
- Selling Digital Products
- Subscription Boxes

Advertising & Sponsorships

- Sponsorships
- Host-Read Ads
- Podcast Advertising Networks
- Podcast Networks
- Website Ad Space
- Newsletter Ads
- Reels / TikToks

Community & Engagement

- Crowdfunding / Listener Donations
- Paid Membership Communities
- Premium Content

Events & Appearances

- Speaking Engagements
- Live Podcast Shows
- Pay-to-Play Guests

Partnerships & Collaborations

- Corporate Partnerships
- Collaborations / Joint Ventures

Audience Growth & Business Leads

- Lead Generation for Your Own Business
- Affiliate Marketing
- Podcast Licensing

Each of these is a viable path—some scalable, some niche, and some perfect for experimental creators.

Personal Monetization Directions

Reflecting on my own journey, here are the paths I've embraced or plan to pursue—each one chosen because it aligns with my values, audience, and long-term vision:

- **Sponsorships:** Partnering with brands that respect the creative relationship I've built with listeners.

- **Merchandising**: Offering branded gear that celebrates fandom and community.
- **Product Reviews**: Collaborating with companies whose offerings genuinely resonate with my niche.
- **Listener Donations**: Inviting direct support to fuel the growth and sustainability of the podcast.
- **Podcast Network Expansion**: Building collective impact and shared resources.
- **Speaking Engagements**: Sharing stories and insights in live, transformative spaces.
- **Live Shows**: Bringing the experience off the feed and into real-time connection.
- **Coaching & Consulting**: Helping emerging creators navigate the landscape I've lived through.
- **Host-Read Ads**: Delivering ad messages with authenticity and clarity.
- **Book Writing**: Documenting this journey and passing on lessons through the written word.

How the Money Moves: PayPal, Deposits, and Sponsor Realities

When you're navigating the world of podcast monetization, it's easy to focus on the *what*—sponsorships, host-read ads, affiliate deals. But just as critical is the *how*: how the money moves, and how creators actually get paid.

For indie podcasters, ad revenue often arrives not through glossy checks or direct deposits, but via digital routes that are familiar, flexible, and creator-friendly. From my own experience and collaborations, here's the breakdown:

Want Sponsors? Here's How to Get Paid

Getting a sponsor feels like a win. But if you're not ready to talk money? You're not ready to monetize.

Let's break down the real-world mechanics that keep your creative business running—and protect your time and talent.

Know the Terms

Before you say yes to any deal, ask:

- **Upfront or Net 30?** Will you get paid before the campaign runs, or 30 days after invoicing?
- **What payment forms are on the table?** PayPal, Venmo, bank transfers, paper checks?
- **Who sets the contract terms?** You... or them? Get comfortable drawing the line—professionally.

Sponsors may love your show, but respect comes from structure. Get your terms in writing.

Where the Money Actually Moves

Let's be real—most indie podcast payments don't arrive with a ribbon and fanfare. Here's how they actually show up:

Method	What to Expect	Real-World Notes
PayPal	Fast and universal	Used in the vast majority of my ad deals. Simple, repeatable, and creator-friendly.
Direct Deposit	Rare but possible	Some mid-sized sponsors use this. Usually tied to formal invoice systems and accounting protocols.
Checks / ACH Transfers	Common with agencies & networks	Slower. Expect formalities, delays, and the occasional "check's in the mail."

💡 ***Pro Tip:*** If you're dealing with grassroots brands or niche sponsors? ***PayPal still rules.***

Protect Yourself

Setting up an LLC adds credibility and helps with taxes and liability. You don't need it on Day One—but it's worth considering as your audience and income scale.

🎙 ***Voice-Forward Advice:*** Ask yourself: *Is this just a hobby—or am I building something with long-term impact?*

Talk Logistics

Sponsors love creators who are clear, professional, and easy to work with. So be ready with:

- Your **rates and deliverables**
- Clear **deadlines** and scheduling expectations
- A clean, simple **invoice system**

A verbal "yes" is great. A paid invoice? *That's the win.*

💡 ***Pro Tip:*** If you're setting up sponsorships, establish payment expectations upfront—ask how they prefer to pay, and clarify timelines. Treat it like any creative contract: friendly, but professional.

A Reality Check

Not every creator secures big sponsorships or premium deals out of the gate. Monetization success hinges on factors like audience size, engagement, timing, and niche.

Small steps matter. Listener donations, affiliate links, and digital products can lay the groundwork while you build trust and consistency.

Lessons from Experience

Our early hosting with BlogTalkRadio and Spreaker's Prime program came at a cost: we had *zero* control over ad loads. One hour might include 10 ads. Three hours? Upwards of 50.

The result? A fragmented listening experience and diluted impact with ads that didn't relate to the programs. We also lost our ability to decide ad categories. Free hosting always comes with a cost, but are you willing to live with it?

We chose independence. We chose control. That's the core lesson—monetization should elevate your work, not exploit it. That's why we use services like RSS.com

Is It Time to Monetize? Run This Audit

- **Audience Engagement**: Is your listener base loyal and growing?
- **Content Maturity**: Is your production polished and consistent?
- **Bandwidth Check**: Can you manage monetization without draining your creative energy?
- **Values Alignment**: Do these strategies reflect who you are and what your brand stands for?

Answer honestly, and you'll gain clarity on where and when to start—or what still needs building.

Market Momentum & What It Means for You

June 2025 marks a tipping point in podcast advertising:

- **91%** of agencies and brands have discussed podcast ad investment
- **78%** are already advertising
- But average quarterly spend is only **$42K**—revealing hesitation

It's momentum without full commitment. And therein lies opportunity.

Tools to Empower You

Most podcast hosts that have dynamic ad insertion give creators a way to prepare for advertiser interest—*some* have minimum download counts and others do not. Submit your link, get in early.

Strategic Advice for Local Advertisers

For hyperlocal brands like car washes:

- Use **geotargeting** to buy impressions precisely
- Leverage **attribution tools** to track ROI beyond promo codes
- Start small, test big—define success before scaling budgets

Reflections to Guide You Forward

- Testing beats guessing
- Clarity of purpose makes experimentation meaningful
- Fear of failure stifles discovery
- Some strategies won't fit your brand—and that's okay

Podcasting offers power and reach—but it demands your intention.

Bridging the Gap: Monetization Meets Infrastructure

So you've explored ways to monetize—maybe even tested a few routes that align with your brand and bandwidth. But sustainable monetization doesn't stand alone. It lives within a system that supports and scales with you. That's where infrastructure comes in: hosting, distribution, web presence, and platform diversification.

If monetization is your message's fuel, your infrastructure is the engine. In the next chapter, we'll build that engine—strategically, creatively, and with your long game in mind.

Chapter 7: Quick Recap — Monetize Without Selling Out

💭 Reflect

- What's your comfort zone (or discomfort zone) around money and creativity?
- Would you still create if monetization wasn't possible?

🎙️ Build

- Choose 2 monetization strategies from the list to experiment with.
- Create a personal "ethics filter" for monetization decisions (audience-first).

🔧 Refine

- Define what "sustainable support" looks like for you—monthly, yearly, emotionally.
- Craft a value statement for your listeners: what they're supporting when they show up.

Chapter 8: Hosting, Distribution, Web Hosting, and Platform Diversification

A Creator's Guide to Choosing What Works

With so many podcasting options out there—and having tested a hefty share over my twenty years in the game—I figured it was time to give a rundown of everything you might encounter. Each platform and tool comes with its own set of strengths and weaknesses, and what works for one creator might feel like a headache to another.

For me, it always comes down to four things: **cost, time, ease of use, and functionality**. Being mostly strapped for cash and balling on a budget, I lean into features I can live with (or live without) depending on the trade-offs. Some platforms offer totally managed solutions, while others require more hands-on effort. And that's the beauty of it—there's no single right answer.

This chapter is your guide to navigating those choices. Whether you're starting from scratch or looking to optimize what you've already built, these hosting platforms, distribution channels, and integration tools will help you shape a setup that fits your workflow and your goals.

Podcast Hosting Platforms

Platform	Description	Personal Experience / Notes
RSS.com	Easy interface and podcast tools	Affiliate code: GCRN
Spreaker	Live and on-demand episodes	Used for dynamic releases
Libsyn	Long-standing hosting solution	Ideal for deep archiving
Buzzsprout	Modern UI and educational resources	Great starter pick
Blubrry	PowerPress plugin integration	Used previously
Castos	Integrates with WordPress	Solid for long-form creators
Podbean	Monetization + mobile tools	Beginner-friendly
Captivate	Marketing and growth tools	Sharp analytics
Riverside	Remote interviews w/high fidelity	Recording-focused platform
RedCircle	Ad monetization + cross-promotion	Built for creators who scale
Transistor.fm	Multi-podcast management	Professional-grade analytics
Simplecast	Enterprise podcast hosting	Excellent UI and metrics
Resonate	Studio-quality hosting + editing	Premium audio support
Zencast	Clean UI and good support	Lightweight solution
OmnyStudios	Enterprise-level hosting	Used by larger networks
Podigee	Multilingual and international reach	Euro-centric distribution

Platform	Description	Personal Experience / Notes
PodServe	Easy setup with built-in marketing	Solo creators approved
Fireside	Clean, privacy-first design	Niche but polished

Distribution Platforms

Platform	Type	Personal Experience / Notes
Apple Podcasts	Directory	Core distribution channel
Spotify	Streaming	Strong engagement and discovery
Player.fm	Aggregator	Used across devices
Amazon Music	Streaming	Easy to onboard
Pandora	Streaming	Less responsive to submissions
TuneIn	Aggregator	Cross-over appeal with radio
iHeartRadio	Network	Legacy brand presence
iTunes	Directory	Tied into Apple's podcast ecosystem
Podchaser	Index	Podcast "IMDb" for episodes and creators
Podcast Index	Open platform	Decentralized for open discovery
RSS.com	Auto-submit	Includes major platforms
Deezer	Streaming	Strong international presence
YouTube Music	Streaming/Video	Great reach and video-podcast support
Spreaker	Distribution	Syncs with platforms

💡 ***Pro Tip:*** *Submit your podcast to every platform possible. Prioritize those with robust user bases, listener reviews, and strong discovery algorithms.*

Why Dedicated Podcast Hosting Beats Website File Storage

It might seem thrifty or clever to stash podcast audio files on your regular website host—but doing so can throttle your growth, compromise reliability, and become a tech headache down the line.

After two decades in the trenches, I've seen plenty of creators hit bandwidth walls, misconfigure RSS feeds, or lose their shows entirely during domain migrations. So let me break it down:

Performance First

Website hosts aren't built for audio delivery—they're optimized for serving text, images, and small assets. Podcast hosting providers, on the other hand, operate content delivery networks (CDNs) that stream and serve audio at scale without bottlenecks or crashes.

Smart Data

Want meaningful analytics? Website hosts might tell you someone downloaded a file. Podcast hosts deliver listener metrics like app usage, geographic location, and completion rates—key data to shape future episodes and pitch to sponsors.

Seamless Syndication

Proper hosting ensures your RSS feed meets the technical specs demanded by Apple Podcasts, Spotify, and other platforms. That includes byte-range support, audio file encoding, and feed hygiene. Most website hosts just can't keep up.

Podcast-First Features

Hosting platforms bake in functionality like:

- Automated RSS feed generation
- Scheduled episode releases
- Audiogram creation
- Integration with directories and apps
- Monetization options

That's a lot to manually wrangle if you're self-hosting through your website.

Risk of Downtime

If your site crashes or your host throttles bandwidth, your podcast may go silent—no streaming, no downloads, no new subscribers. Podcast hosts are purpose-built to maintain uptime and continuity, even during traffic spikes.

Hosting your podcast on a specialized platform isn't just a tech upgrade—it's a creator safeguard. It's like preserving your best comics in a climate-controlled vault instead of stacking them next to the water heater. Sure, it costs a few bucks, but it protects the legacy you're building.

Website Hosting for Podcasts

Traditional Web Hosting Providers

If you're building your podcast hub with WordPress, consider these options for reliability, price, and flexibility.

Web Host	Description	Notes
Hostinger	Feature-rich WordPress hosting	Strong performance and value *Affiliate link – Promo Code: GCRN10*
Bluehost	Budget-friendly WP hosting	Accessible and beginner-friendly
WordPress.com	Integrated WP hosting	Simplified setup—no external host needed

Podcast-Specific Website Hosting Platforms

Want an all-in-one platform with podcast-first features? These options skip the WordPress route and give you fast, branded websites with built-in podcast tools.

Platform	Website Features	Notes & Highlights
Captivate	Customizable podcast website	Growth tools, email integration, private podcasting
Alitu	Recording + publishing + transcripts	Beginner-friendly workflow automation
Castos	Site builder + WP plugin	Private feeds, SSR integration via Seriously Simple
Podpage	Auto-generates podcast website	No coding, SEO tools, call-to-action widgets

Platform	Website Features	Notes & Highlights
Simplecast	Fully functional site w/custom domain	Advanced analytics, marketing widgets
Podbean	Free podcast website	Video podcast support, monetization tools
Transistor	Branded website per show	Multi-show management and private feeds
RedCircle	Monetized site + team tools	Built for podcast growth and scaling

Podcast Websites

If you want concierge-style service and branding support, Podcast Websites offers a fully managed podcast platform.

Service	Description	Notes
Podcast Websites	Website + media hosting + branding tools	SEO, email capture, membership funnels, live support

Choosing the Right Website Strategy

Use this quick breakdown to decide what suits your workflow:

Option	Best For
WordPress + Hosting	Full customization, plugin control, long-term growth
Podcast-Specific Platforms	All-in-one convenience with podcast-first focus
Podcast Websites	High-touch setup, branding support, built-in marketing

🧠 ***Reflect On:***

- Do you want more control or less maintenance?
- Will your site support more than just episodes (blogs, merch, memberships)?
- Are you managing one show or multiple podcasts?

Chapter 8: Quick Recap — Pick the Tech That Works

🗨 Reflect

- Which platforms or hosts align with your workflow and goals?
- Are you optimizing for simplicity, scale, or flexibility?

🎙 Build

- List current tech tools. Highlight gaps and priorities for upgrades.
- Decide: do you want a WordPress site, podcast-specific host, or concierge solution?

🔧 Refine

- Draft a platform comparison chart based on your needs.
- Choose one system to set up in the next 7 days—website, host, or channel.

Chapter 9: Website Integration, Community Engagement, and Brand Legacy

Where Your Podcast Lives Beyond the Feed

Once your infrastructure is set, your website becomes the heartbeat of your brand. It's where listeners go to connect, learn more about the hosts, share feedback, and explore your back catalog. It's also the home base for building a loyal, engaged community.

Whether you're building from scratch or refining what already exists, this chapter covers everything from WordPress integrations to listener activation strategies—and how your creative presence becomes a lasting legacy.

WordPress Website Essentials

Based on hands-on experience, here's what I recommend to optimize your site for performance, presentation, and long-term brand strategy.

Recommended Plugins

Plugin	Function	Notes
Seriously Simple Podcasting	Feed + player + metadata	Clean and reliable; can be integrated with Captivate
PowerPress by Blubrry	Podcast feed and player	Allows self-hosting, but advanced features tied to Blubrry

Plugin	Function	Notes
Podcast Importer SecondLine	Migrate multi-show episodes	Ideal for multi-show setups
Auto YouTube Importer	Sync video episodes to site posts	Cross-media compatibility
Seriously Simple Speakers	Add host bios to episodes	Adds personality and transparency
Seriously Simple Stats	On-site episode traffic analytics	Optional—good if host doesn't provide page-level data
Thrive Comments	Social login-based commenting system	More control and speed than DISQUS
Jetpack	Performance, backup, and engagement tools	Not essential, but useful for all-in-one functionality
Yoast SEO	Optimize site structure for discovery	Great for organic search visibility
WPForms / Forminator	Listener feedback forms and contact capture	Choose based on UI preference
Pretty Links	Affiliate link and promo tracking	Must-have for marketing and monetization

Recommended Themes

Theme	Features	Notes
WpCasterPro	Built for podcasts and blog content	Your current favorite—clean and podcast-centered
Jannah	Entertainment site-ready, visual storytelling	Excellent for pop culture and media-heavy projects
Astra	Lightweight, performance-driven	Great for custom branding

Theme	Features	Notes
OceanWP	Responsive with media flexibility	Solid design versatility
Neve	Fast, minimalist, and mobile-friendly	Ideal for streamlined podcast blogs
Hello Elementor	Full page builder support	Drag-and-drop customizable
SecondLine Themes	Podcast-specific aesthetic and integration	Pairs well with their plugins (Speakers, Importers)

Artwork & Episode Prep

Your visuals are your podcast's front porch—a welcoming space that says, "Come in, this is worth your time." Whether it's your show logo, episode thumbnails, or social graphics, cohesive and intentional artwork boosts discoverability and reinforces your brand identity across platforms.

Here's how to design visuals that resonate, without overwhelming your workflow:

Graphic Allies for Creators

Tool	Use Case	Notes
Canva	Cover art, episode graphics, social posts	Drag-and-drop editor; freemium; ideal for fast turnaround
Adobe Spark	Banners, animated visuals, promo templates	Lightweight; easy export for social platforms
Adobe Illustrator	Logos, vector branding, layered graphics	Industry-grade; great for long-term consistency

💡 **Pro Tip:** Episode graphics can double as social media posts. Use Canva templates to create series-specific designs for YouTube thumbnails, audiograms, or guest quotes. Build once, resize forever.

Apple Podcasts Artwork Requirements

If you plan to syndicate on Apple Podcasts (and you should—it's a primary discovery platform), your show artwork needs to meet these specs:

Requirement	Description
Size	3000 x 3000 pixels
Format	JPG or PNG
Color Profile	RGB (not CMYK)
File Size	Under 500 KB preferred
Safe Zone Tip	Keep title/logo centered to avoid cropping

Why It Matters:

Your artwork appears in podcast directories, apps, social previews, and embedded players. If your image is blurry, off-center, or doesn't scale well, you miss a chance to make a lasting first impression.

Quick Checklist for Visual Prep:

- ✅ Title and tagline readable at thumbnail size
- ✅ Fonts match brand tone and podcast theme
- ✅ Colors optimized for screen—not print
- ✅ Logo or imagery centered for mobile visibility

💬 Listener Engagement Tips

Building an audience is just the first step. Keeping them engaged is the foundation of growth. Here's what works:

- Ask questions during episodes to spark dialogue
- Run contests tied to show themes or milestones
- Use social media to share audio clips, behind-the-scenes content, or listener shoutouts
- Highlight user reviews and listener emails during episodes
- Build spaces like Discord servers, Patreon hubs, or Facebook Groups to create a hangout zone

Let your listeners become contributors—not just consumers. Give them a reason to return, recommend, and repost.

Project Feedback Practices

The best feedback loops are intentional, honest, and fueled by collaboration. Here's how to refine your show with purpose:

- **Solicit feedback** from trusted listeners, creators, or collaborators
- **Research your podcast name** across domains and platforms before launch
- **Define your "why"**—your purpose, voice, and value proposition
- **Publish consistently**, evolve openly, and **celebrate creative wins** (even the small ones)

You don't need to be perfect out of the gate. You just need to be progressing—with clarity.

Pitch Perfect: Getting Press Coverage That Matters

When it comes to podcast growth, press coverage is a level-up move that most creators overlook—either because it feels intimidating, or they assume it's reserved for big-budget shows backed by corporations. The truth? It's totally achievable. You just need to know how to pitch it right.

Industry pros have pulled back the curtain on what it takes to get your podcast reviewed by the media. Their full breakdown lives here, and trust me—it's required reading if you're serious about visibility, credibility, and maybe even landing network deals.

Here's a turbocharged version of their advice:

Why Press Matters

- Visibility for your show = new listeners.
- Credibility for you = future sponsors and guest requests.
- Local press = speaking gigs and recognition in your own backyard.

🎙️ ***Voice-Forward Advice:*** Example—GeekCast Radio Network received a flurry of attention when we hit our 15-year milestone. A simple press release sparked local coverage and opened doors for speaking opportunities. Never underestimate how press can amplify your voice—even outside podcasting circles.

Finding the Right People

- Research outlets and writers who've covered your genre.
- Research outlets, media and print organizations in your local market.
- Use tools like Muckrack, RocketReach, and GreatPods to build contact lists.
- Subscribe to industry newsletters like *Podnews, Sounds Profitable, Podcast Tonight, Amplifi Media, The DWNLOAD with Chris Peterson, Vulture's 1.5x Speed*, and *Inside Podcasting.*

Crafting the Pitch

- Keep it under 250 words.
- Personalize your outreach (refer to their work).
- Include links, artwork, and a press kit.
- Make it timely, relevant, and newsworthy.
- End with a clear CTA: "Would you consider reviewing our show?" or "We'd love to be featured."

Common Pitfalls to Dodge

- Mass-emailing generic pitches = instant delete.
- Watch your subject line. Under 7 words is best.
- Don't ghost after sending—follow up kindly.
- Be human. Be helpful. Don't be pushy.

After You Land Coverage

- Share it across your channels.
- Thank the writer publicly and personally.

- Add it to your podcast description, website, and media kit.

Relationship-building isn't a one-time game. It's a creative ecosystem. Whether you're indie or network-backed, press done thoughtfully can be the oxygen your show needs.

Building Brand Legacy

Your podcast isn't just a series of episodes—it's a mosaic of values, relationships, and moments. Here's how to craft the legacy you want to leave behind:

- **Define your mission** and let it drive everything—content, tone, partnerships
- **Stick to your values**, even when trends tempt you to pivot
- **Celebrate milestones** with your audience and team
- **Pay it forward**—mentor up-and-comers, share hard-earned wisdom, and lift other voices when you can

Legacy isn't built in downloads; it's built in impact.

Chapter 9: Quick Recap — Build the Space Between Episodes

💭 **Reflect**

- Does your website echo your brand's personality—visually and functionally?
- Are your listeners just tuning in—or truly connecting with your world?

🎨 **Visualize**

- Audit your podcast artwork for clarity, brand alignment, and platform readiness (Apple specs included).
- Choose one design tool—Canva, Spark, or Illustrator—and create episode graphics that reinforce your show's identity.

💬 **Engage**

- Build an interaction plan: listener comments, polls, Discord invites, or shoutouts during episodes.
- Launch one visual-driven campaign (a contest, quote series, or guest spotlight) using your new artwork toolkit.

🔧 **Refine**

- Activate plugins that enhance site usability and community engagement.
- Update your homepage or bio with a "brand moment" that reflects your podcast's purpose and tone.

Chapter 10: Evolve Without Burning Out

Creator Wellness, Sustainable Growth, and the Future of Podcasting

Podcasting isn't just publishing—it's personal. It's late-night edits, the invisible weight of burnout, and the quiet victory of hitting "upload" when you almost didn't. If growth is the goal, wellness must be the fuel.

Burnout doesn't show up with flashing lights. It creeps in with silence.

Recognizing Burnout

Burnout is a silent thief. It rarely crashes in with alarms—it slips under the door with fatigue, doubt, and detachment. Sometimes it sounds like skipping your favorite segment. Sometimes it looks like staring at your timeline for an hour and moving nothing.

That's creative depletion. And it deserves your attention.

Here's what it might look like:

- **Physical:** Constant fatigue, headaches, disrupted sleep
- **Emotional:** Irritability, feeling overwhelmed or creatively numb

- **Behavioral:** Procrastination, reduced output, ghosting your own work

Burnout isn't always loud. But it always demands recognition.

Setting Realistic Expectations

Longevity isn't about hustle—it's about clarity.

- **Define success** by your personal values—not the comparison trap.
- **Prioritize joy-makers, not just task lists.**
- **Schedule breaks**—not as a reward, but as routine maintenance.
- **Celebrate the small wins.** They're the true fuel.

Ask yourself: **What does creative fatigue sound like in your life—and how can you answer it gently, not with guilt?**

Adaptive Workflows

Burnout isn't the enemy. Rigidity is.

The more your show evolves, the more your systems should stretch with you. Here's what sustainable structure looks like:

- A DAW template that trims editing hours
- A "just-in-case" solo episode when guests fall through
- A scheduled day off from metrics and mirrors
- A Trello board that maps out joy—not just deadlines

And beyond that:

- **Streamline** tasks that drain energy
- **Leverage tech** like Descript or Auphonic to cut friction
- **Delegate when possible.** Trust your collaborators to carry part of the signal

Automation's great—but don't let it flatten your voice. Personalize what you batch. Review what you schedule. Use systems to support soul—not substitute for it.

Iterate, Don't Idolize Perfection

Mistakes aren't failures. They're field notes.

- Edit with compassion.
- Launch with humanity.
- Shift when the joy disappears—and return when the purpose is clearer.

Sustainability isn't just about keeping up. It's about knowing when to slow down, zoom out, and protect the flame.

Generational Bridges

You don't have to reinvent your roots—you just need to make them relatable. Connecting across generations makes your content richer and your brand more inclusive.

80s/90s Geek Roots Meet Gen Z Curiosity

- Lean into shared interests: gaming, gadgets, pop culture
- Storytelling bridges nostalgia with modern themes

- Partner with younger creators to exchange perspectives

Bringing Nostalgia Forward Without Gatekeeping

- Share your geeky past like an open book, not a closed club
- Let the past inform, not dominate, current creativity
- Create bridges instead of boundaries—invite younger voices in

Mentoring the Next Wave of Audio Storytellers

- Share what you've learned, flaws included
- Uplift creators experimenting with new formats
- Build community around growth—not hierarchy

The Future Is Personal

Podcasting keeps evolving—but connection still wins. AI and automation are tools. Your voice is the soul.

AI, Automation, and the Power of the Human Voice

- Use tech to spark creativity, not replace it
- Keep storytelling rooted in truth and emotion
- Blend innovation with intimacy for a powerful listener experience

Why Podcasts Are More Than "Content"

- Build relationships, not just playlists

- Deliver impact through education, empathy, and entertainment
- Showcase a variety of voices—listeners want to hear themselves in the story too

Blending Intimacy with Innovation

- Stay personal, even when experimenting
- Try new formats, platforms, or tech—but tie them back to your brand
- Future-proof by staying values-driven—not just trend-conscious

Chapter 10: Quick Recap — Protect the Flame

💭 Reflect

- What does creative fatigue look like in your world—and how do you respond to it?
- When was the last time you created with joy, not just obligation?

🎙 Build

- Identify one system that needs simplification or support.
- Choose a recurring rest ritual—monthly, weekly, or micro—before burnout calls the shots.

🔧 Refine

- Redesign one part of your workflow to honor energy, not output.
- Draft your creative wellness check-in: what to ask yourself before every recording week.

Chapter 11: Expanding the Ecosystem

Cross-Platform Synergy, Brand Values, and Purposeful Growth

Your creative journey isn't limited to a single channel or format—it's a living ecosystem. Audio, video, text, and community all play a part in how your brand is experienced and remembered. This chapter explores how to expand with intention, connect across platforms, and build an ecosystem that reflects your values and evolves with your audience.

Cross-Platform Synergy

Audio, Video, Text, and Community

Building momentum requires layers—content that overlaps, connects, and enhances the overall experience.

- **Layered Content**: Repurpose and interconnect podcasts, blog posts, videos, and social clips to increase discovery and deepen engagement
- **Unified Branding**: Keep your tone, visuals, and messaging consistent across all platforms
- **Community Integration**: Extend the listener experience into forums, Discord servers, live streams, or social channels where conversations happen

Think of each format as a different doorway to your brand—and the more aligned they are, the more immersive the experience.

Monetization Woven Into Storytelling

Monetization shouldn't feel like a detour—it should feel like a natural extension of the story you're telling.

- **Authentic Integration**: Talk about your offerings the way you talk about anything important—honestly and clearly
- **Value-Driven Offers**: Align sponsorships, affiliate recommendations, and merchandise with audience needs
- **Collaborative Ventures**: Partner with brands or creators that amplify your voice rather than dilute it

Treat monetization not as an add-on, but as part of your story's structure.

Brand Values Guiding the Ecosystem

Honesty, Innovation, Fun, and More

When your values drive the system, everything clicks—collaborations, content decisions, community tone.

- **Core Principles**: Make your values part of every decision, from headlines to partnerships
- **Audience Trust**: Be transparent. Invite feedback. Own your mistakes. Celebrate together.

- **Creative Experimentation**: Don't play it safe—just play it true. Test formats, themes, partnerships while keeping your compass calibrated

Your audience doesn't just want content. They want content that feels like it came from someone they believe in.

Managing Growth With Purpose

Scaling Without Noise

More isn't always better. When it comes to growth, quality, clarity, and sustainability win.

- **Strategic Expansion**: Add platforms and content types with intent, not just visibility
- **Audience-Centric Decisions**: Let feedback and behavior guide what gets doubled-down
- **Sustainable Practices**: Protect your creative bandwidth. Choose processes that honor your mental health and your message.

Growth can be exciting—or it can be overwhelming. The difference is purpose.

Why Growth Looks Different in 2025

Here's the twist: The fastest-growing podcasts this year aren't cranking out episodes like it's 2010. They're dialing in quality over quantity—experimenting, streamlining, and refusing to burn out for the feed gods.

Video-first creators are carving out space on YouTube, not just chasing trends but shaping them. And guess what? No mega budgets, no ad blitzes. Just audience engagement, organic momentum, and content that sticks.

The latest reports show:

- Median downloads per episode are up 10.4%
- YouTube has officially jumped over Instagram as the top growth channel
- The best shows are rethinking format—ditching predictable interviews for creative hybrids and episodic arcs

This isn't just "pivot to video"—it's pivot to purpose. If you're still publishing weekly out of obligation, stop. **Experiment. Share it. Refine as you go**. Because strategic innovation beats brute-force scheduling every time.

💬 **Real talk?** I've lived both ends of that spectrum—the burnout of "more = better," and the calm of "less but sharper." The second one's where the magic happens.

Your Brand as a Living Organism

This ecosystem isn't rigid—it's adaptive. The format might shift. The platforms might evolve. But the spirit stays true.

By treating your brand like a living organism, you build something resilient, engaging, and entirely yours—a system that thrives on synergy, values, and purpose.

Chapter 11: Quick Recap — Expand with Intention

💭 Reflect

- Are you growing for reach—or for resonance?
- What part of your creative presence feels aligned with your voice, and what feels borrowed?
- Does your content ecosystem reflect your values across platforms, or just your output?

🎙️ Build

- Start small: remix one episode into a video short, blog post, or Discord thread.
- Map your brand across platforms—what doors are open, and where is the story incomplete?
- Choose one community engagement path: feedback form, shout-out segment, or listener question box.

🔧 Refine

- Audit your platforms and visuals for tone, consistency, and clarity.
- Pick one system to simplify—tech stack, scheduling, or collaborator workflow.
- Define what sustainable growth looks like for you: intentional, values-led, and audience-aware.

Chapter 12: Purpose-Driven Creation

The Signal You Follow—When Systems Fade

The chapters before this focused on outward momentum—platforms, partnerships, and strategies for building something bold and sustainable. But amid all the systems and synergy, there's a quieter rhythm that hums underneath it all. You know it. It's that feeling when a story lands right. When a listener sends a message that reminds you why you started. When the mic feels less like a tool and more like home.

What fuels this journey isn't just your tech stack or branding—it's that elusive mix of passion and presence. It's what keeps you up at night editing, and what draws you back even when metrics dip or burnout whispers.

Let's take a moment to tune back into that signal.

Clarifying Your Why

You didn't start podcasting just to fill airtime. There was a reason you stepped up to the mic—something deeper than algorithms and gear. Let's reconnect with it.

- **What Keeps You Coming Back**: Reflect on the moments that renew your energy
- **Origin Shapes Mission**: Let your beginnings inform the values you carry forward

- **Align Personal Purpose with Community Value**: Meet your listeners where your story and their needs overlap

Creative Integrity in a Noisy World

The digital landscape can pull you in a dozen directions at once. Staying grounded is a creative act in itself.

- **Say No to Trends That Don't Fit**: Ignore hype that dilutes your message
- **Honor Your Voice When Metrics Dip**: Authenticity doesn't always spike analytics
- **Know When to Pivot vs. Plant Roots**: Balance evolution with essence

The Long Game

Purpose isn't measured in downloads—it's built through intention, consistency, and lasting resonance.

- **Build with Patience**: Sustainable growth beats fleeting virality
- **Create for Legacy**: Focus on impact, not just reach
- **Show Up Consistently**: Small actions compound over time

Aligning Purpose Across Platforms

What flows outward must also flow inward. Once your purpose is clear, it should infuse how you show up across every platform—not just what you post, but why you post it.

Purpose as Creative Compass

- Lead with feeling, not format—let the story dictate the shape it takes
- Use each platform to deepen, not just repeat, the connection
- Measure impact by resonance, not reach

Expressive Consistency

- Tone and vibe matter more than visuals alone—be recognizable by voice, not just logo
- Reuse content, yes—but remix it with heart to match each space
- Let your values guide what you *don't* post as much as what you do

From Noise to Signal

- A TikTok clip, a blog post, a Discord AMA—each is a chance to echo your "why," not just your brand
- If you stopped posting tomorrow, would your presence still feel honest and complete?

Ethical Creation and Influence

You have influence—and with it comes responsibility. This isn't about being perfect. It's about being clear.

- **Transparency in Partnerships**: Let listeners in on how collaborations work

- **Serve Over Self-Promote**: Build trust by making audience value a priority

- **Be a Voice for Something**: Speak from conviction, not just commentary

When It's Time to Pause

Rest is resistance to burnout. Redirection is part of progress. You're allowed to stop—and still succeed.

- **Recognize Seasons of Rest**: Know when to slow down
- **Give Yourself Permission to Shift**: Redefine the path when needed
- **Create Sustainably**: Build workflows that nurture rather than drain

Expanding the Ecosystem

From Purpose to Platform Synergy

Once your purpose is clear, it fuels everything around it—from how you communicate to how you grow.

Cross-Platform Synergy

- **Layered Content**: Connect your podcast, video, blog, and community into one experience
- **Unified Branding**: Keep your tone, voice, and values consistent everywhere
- **Community Integration**: Make your listeners part of the ecosystem—forums, Discord, social chat, and live sessions

Monetization Woven Into Storytelling

- **Authentic Integration**: Let monetization reflect—not redirect—your mission
- **Value-Driven Offers**: Products, memberships, and partners should match what your audience genuinely needs
- **Collaborative Ventures**: Amplify reach through aligned partnerships, not just reach for numbers

Brand Values as the Backbone

- **Core Principles**: Infuse your brand with honesty, creativity, and joy
- **Build Audience Trust**: Be transparent, consistent, and human
- **Experiment Creatively**: Push limits while staying true to your compass

Managing Growth With Purpose

- **Strategic Expansion**: Grow thoughtfully—less noise, more clarity
- **Audience-Centric Decisions**: Use feedback and intuition to guide your next move
- **Sustainable Practices**: Create space for rest, revision, and long-term creativity

Your brand isn't static—it's a living rhythm. Every choice echoes your values. Every piece of content invites connection. By honoring your purpose at every level—from mic to monetization—you build something with impact, integrity, and soul.

Chapter 12: Quick Recap — Reconnect with the Why

💭 **Reflect**

- What stories feel like yours to tell right now?
- Are you creating from clarity or obligation?

🎙 **Build**

- Rewrite your mission statement—no fluff, just truth
- Send one honest message to your audience about your creative journey

🔧 **Refine**

- Reassess your episode structure—is it serving your message?
- Choose one action this week that restores joy in the process

Chapter 13: Passing the Torch

Mentorship and Creative Legacy

There comes a point when podcasting isn't just about producing episodes—it's about what those episodes *do* for people. For me, it's no longer just about showing up to record; it's about showing up to lead, teach, and build something that lasts beyond my own mic.

Over the past few years, I've found myself in a new chapter—less driven by downloads, more drawn to the ripple effect of mentorship. From podcast groups like **The RSS Space**, to connecting with youth through **Boys and Girls Clubs**, giving back via **Kiwanis**, contributing to the **Loveland Reporter-Herald**, shaping thoughts on **LinkedIn**, and collaborating with peers—I've embraced this role not just as a creator, but as a guide.

It's about value over vanity. Yes, podcasting can entertain. But in a world flooded with advice—some of it great—some of it is self-serving, predatory, or diluted with false promises—what stands out is **authentic experience**. It's not about being the next Joe Rogan. It's about helping someone avoid the missteps you learned the hard way. That's the heart of the legacy I want to leave.

Why Mentorship Matters

- **Empowering the Next Generation**: Mentorship isn't top-down—it's hands-on. It's about showing others they can create something meaningful with the tools already within reach.

- **The Joy of Experience**: Sharing what you've learned—both successes and setbacks—is deeply rewarding.
- **Ripple Effects**: A well-timed insight can change the course of a creator's path. Sometimes they'll tell you. Sometimes you'll never know.

Your Journey as a Mentor

- **Lessons Learned**: From recording late-night episodes to navigating distribution chaos, these scars taught me more than any tutorial ever could.
- **What You Wish You Knew**: Like how not every fancy tool is necessary. Or that "perfect audio" means nothing without emotional resonance.
- **Supporting New Voices**: Mentorship means helping someone shape *their* voice—not cloning yours. I try to lead with flexibility, not formulas.

Developing a Mentorship Mindset

- **Listening Over Lecturing**: Sometimes creators don't need answers—they need someone to listen as they find them.
- **Asking Thoughtful Questions**: "What does success mean to you?" often reveals more than any technical tip.
- **Encouraging Experimentation**: Not every idea will land—but every attempt is a step forward.

Mentorship Models for Creators

Model	Description	Example Contexts
1-on-1 Coaching	Personalized feedback and support	Zoom calls, in-person sessions
Peer-Led Communities	Support through shared experience	Discord groups, LinkedIn audio forums
Internships/Collabs	Learn-by-doing opportunities	Co-productions, behind-the-scenes workshops
Educational Content	Books, guides, events that democratize access	*Altered Audio*, local podcast meetups

💡 ***Pro Tip:*** You don't need to be everywhere. You just need to show up with intention—where it counts.

Legacy Effect: Mentorship That Echoes

- **Sharing Your Journey**: A recorded episode is powerful. But documenting *why* you made it? That's lasting.
- **Planting Seeds**: Mentorship isn't instant. It's slow growth, silent roots, and future fruit.
- **The Invisible Audience**: Whether in DMs or on Discord, someone out there is listening and learning—even if you never hear from them.

Celebrating Independent Voices

Give Credit Generously

Your mic reaches people—but your voice isn't the only one that matters. Elevating independent creators is one of the most powerful things you can do.

- Shout out the podcasters who inspired your style
- Name the small creators who shaped your fandom
- Promote indie guests, cross-post their work, and tag them thoughtfully
- Cite your influences—legacy deserves lineage

You were lifted by those who came before you. Pass it on.

Mentorship isn't the end of creating. It's the extension of it. The echoes of your journey become a guide for someone else's.

By choosing to pass the torch, you don't just give others a path forward. You build something that reflects your values, your voice, and your belief that content should *mean* something.

Chapter 13: Quick Recap — Pass the Mic

💭 **Reflect**

- Who lifted you when you started? Who could you lift now?
- Are you mentoring by accident... or intention?

🎙️ **Build**

- Write a simple outreach message to a creator you admire
- Design your mentorship model: 1-on-1, community, educational content?

🔧 **Refine**

- Highlight an independent voice publicly this month
- Set one long-term legacy goal—and take a step toward it today

Chapter 14: The Next Frontier

Vision, Impact, and the Rhythm of What Comes Next

The creative path never ends—it just shifts shape. It evolves from spark to rhythm, from solo act to signal, from passion project to platform. As I've grown alongside this medium, my role has expanded from host and producer to mentor, collaborator, and teacher.

These days, the frontier looks different. It's not just new tech or global reach—it's about building legacy through *connection*. Not by chasing attention, but by crafting momentum that inspires others to create on their own terms.

Exploring New Horizons

- **Emerging Technologies**: AI tools, immersive formats, and remote collaboration have transformed the creative workflow. The signal isn't limited to a mic—it lives in every medium we shape.
- **Global Collaboration**: Whether it's cross-border podcast co-ops or LinkedIn voice chats, creators are finding new ways to amplify one another across geographies.
- **Sustainable Practices**: Growth that honors our mental health, creative bandwidth, and personal lives is no longer optional—it's the new blueprint.

The Power of Storytelling

- **Universal Themes**: Geek culture, identity, and personal triumphs resonate far beyond niche audiences. Storytelling is how we bridge generations, interests, and beliefs.
- **Innovative Formats**: Interactive episodes, video shorts, VR podcast lounges—the future is here, and it's modular.
- **Impactful Messages**: Whether discussing social issues or celebrating fandoms, creators now hold the power to inform, advocate, and inspire.

Building a Legacy

- **Mentorship**: I've found the greatest joy not in producing content, but in helping others *skip steps* I had to stumble through. Whether it's podcast bootcamps with the RSS Space, youth programs via Kiwanis or Boys and Girls Clubs, or LinkedIn mentorship threads—it's about passing the torch.
- **Community Engagement**: Listeners aren't just fans. They're collaborators, cheerleaders, and trusted peers. My work with Loveland's creative groups reminds me that local voices matter just as much as viral ones.
- **Creative Integrity**: The future will challenge our values. The tools may evolve—but staying grounded in purpose and authenticity will keep the signal strong.

Chapter 14: Quick Recap — The Signal Carries Forward

💭 Reflect

- What does creative legacy look like in your world?
- What signal will your audience carry long after the episode ends?

🎙️ Build

- Define your vision for the next frontier—one sentence, one goal
- Create a legacy manifesto: platform, values, mentorship, impact

🔧 Refine

- Choose one story, product, or project to plant this season
- Share your "why now" publicly—or at least write it somewhere visible

Epilogue: The Signal Lives On

This isn't a goodbye—it's a frequency shift.

The signal doesn't end here. It evolves with every creator who picks up the mic, every listener who finds resonance, and every story that echoes across time zones, forums, and timelines.

Whether you've just hit record or you're 200+ episodes deep—your voice matters. Your perspective, geeky quirks and all, adds nuance to a creative landscape that desperately needs more of it.

So, keep creating. Keep listening. Keep amplifying. Let the signal live through you.

Postscript: From the Desk of Steve Megatron

To everyone who hit play, left a comment, joined the convo, or simply nodded along on your morning drive—thank you.

This book isn't a roadmap. It's a handshake. It's me saying, "Hey, I've been where you are. You're not alone."

If you're holding this book, you're part of the signal now. Whether you're creating, mentoring, experimenting, or simply soaking it all in—your voice matters.

So go. Make something that echoes. Unleash the Geek in YOU™—and let the voice grow.

Creator Identity & Professional Background

Who I Am, When the Mic's Off

I've worn many hats—sometimes at the same time: online host, producer, tech enthusiast, designer, and voice actor. For the past 20 years, podcasting has been my creative playground, career path, and connection point.

My background blends:

- 🎙️ Voiceover and narration for multiple web series, podcasts and corporate recordings.
- 🎧 Podcast appearances across *GeekCast Radio Network, All Things Transformers, Altered Geek, Movie Week in REview, The Podcasters Roundtable*, *The Dragon's Lair*, *This Week in Geek*, and many others.
- 🖥️ Guest hosting and event work with the Michigan Science Center, including Star Trek Night.
- 🧠 Thought leadership through LinkedIn and community presentations like the Transformers convention, Iacon Online. And multiple local organizations that want to discover podcasting for the first time.
- ✍️ Articles for Lifewire Tech and Komando.

- 💻 Design and web strategy behind GeekCast Radio Network's evolving identity

At every step, I've chased work that aligns with what I love: entertainment, tech, voice, educating and creative mentorship. If there's a thread that ties it all together—it's curiosity.

Acknowledgments

To the GCRN crew—thank you for building our network with each podcast episode released.

To co-founder TFG1Mike—your belief and partnership gave this idea its first heartbeat and continues to do so today.

To our listeners—you're not just the audience. You're the reason we keep recording and who we love having conversations with.

To the geek creators out there—make waves. Make noise. Make it count. Entertain, educate, and provide authentic content with value.

And to my younger self—you had no idea where this mic would lead, but you turned it on anyway. That was enough.

The Creator's Manifesto

Unleash the Geek in You™ — A Rally Cry for the Passionate and Persistent

- Create with Purpose
- Honor the Process
- Value Every Listener
- Speak What Matters
- Stay Curious
- Lead with Kindness
- Protect Your Joy
- Mentor the Next Wave
- Think Long Game
- Unleash the Geek in YOU™: Loudly. Proudly. Relentlessly.

☑ The Signal Sync Checklist

A Tactical Tuning Guide for New & Veteran Creators

✅ **Define your show's creative identity *(Ch. 1–3)*** Own your voice—flaws and all. Craft a format that reflects your personality and purpose.

✅ **Shape your show's format and tone *(Ch. 4)*** Solo, interview, or hybrid—find what amplifies your story. Test your mic setup and record your first message.

✅ **Polish your visual brand *(Ch. 9)*** Design cover art and episode thumbnails with Canva, Spark, or Illustrator. Hit Apple specs for podcast directories.

✅ **Choose 2 monetization models to pilot *(Ch. 7)*** Plan your payment logistics with confidence. Define what sustainable support looks like for you.

✅ **Set your cadence and backup workflows *(Ch. 4 & 9)*** Build repeatable templates and systems that protect your time, joy, and creativity.

✅ **Reflect on your purpose before checking metrics *(Ch. 12)*** Reconnect with your "why." Define your mission statement and realign platforms accordingly.

✅ **Draft a podcast press kit *(Appendix)*** Bio, description, social links, logo, key episodes—ready for outreach and visibility.

✅ **Bookmark mentorship tools & templates *(Ch. 11–13)*** Collab one-pagers, outreach scripts, and interview request formats—pay it forward.

✅ **Choose your website platform *(Ch. 8–9)*** Whether WordPress, Captivate, or Podpage, pick a space that reflects your brand and invites engagement.

✅ **Review your brand tone and graphic style *(Ch. 9 & Checklist)*** Use the Brand Voice Checklist to define your vibe—playful, geeky, authoritative, bold.

✅ **Schedule monthly strategy reviews *(Ch. 14)*** Take stock. Refocus. Reconnect. Let the rhythm evolve as your podcast does.

✅ **Print and sign your Creator's Manifesto *(Appendix)*** Tape it above your mic. Let it guide the frequency. Create with purpose, not perfection.

Start Here Checklist

Practical Momentum for Beginning Your Journey

- Define Your Goals
- Identify Your Audience
- Choose Your Platforms
- Set a Schedule
- Gather Resources
- Start Small
- Track Progress
- Stay Inspired

Resources Appendix

Tools, Platforms, Articles, and Favorite Picks

Explore More from the Signal

- **GeekCast Radio Network** Your legacy, your library, your launchpad. Community-driven, culture-powered podcasting.
- **RSS.com** Podcast hosting, analytics, and monetization—tools that keep creators in control. **Use promo code: GCRN**

Glossary Index

Term	Definition
DAW (Digital Audio Workstation)	Software used for recording, editing, and mixing audio (e.g., Audacity, Adobe Audition)
RSS Feed	A stream of data that lets podcast platforms syndicate your episodes automatically
Normalization	The process of adjusting audio levels so volume remains consistent across a track or episode
Levelating	A legacy term popularized by the "Levelator" app—refers to automatic leveling of spoken-word audio
Compression	An effect used to balance loud and soft parts of audio, creating smoother sound
EQ (Equalization)	Adjusting frequency ranges (bass, mids, treble) to improve vocal clarity and tone
Multitrack Recording	Capturing each speaker or sound source on a separate audio track for clean editing

Term	Definition
ID3 Tags	Metadata embedded in audio files (title, artist, description) used by podcast apps
Binaural Audio	Recording style that simulates 3D sound perception when listening with headphones
Clipping	Audio distortion caused when volume exceeds the maximum recording threshold
Show Notes	Written summary accompanying an episode—includes topics, links, and timestamps
Feedburner / Redirect	Tools or links used to reroute RSS feeds (especially when changing podcast hosts)
Cardioid Mic	Microphone pickup pattern that captures sound mainly from the front (ideal for solo recording)

Recommended Tools and Platforms

Tool / Platform	Description
Canva	Design podcast covers, social graphics, and branding elements
Audacity	Free, open-source audio editing software
Adobe Audition	Pro-level podcast editing and mastering suite
Hostinger	WordPress web hosting with strong feature set – Promo code – *GCRN10*
Seriously Simple Podcasting	WordPress plugin for managing podcast feeds and episodes
PowerPress by Blubrry	Advanced podcast plugin (best when paired with Blubrry hosting)
Podcast Importer by SecondLine	Import episodes from other platforms (free & pro versions)
Auto YouTube Importer	Sync YouTube videos to your WordPress site
Seriously Simple Speakers	Add hosts and bios to episode pages
Thrive Comments	Comment system with social login integrations
Jetpack	Performance, backups, and engagement tools for WordPress
Pretty Links	Track affiliate links and campaigns

Tool / Platform	Description
WPForms / Forminator	Easy-to-use form builders for listener feedback
Discord	Create private or public communities for listener engagement
Patreon	Build membership models and offer exclusive content
RSS.com	Podcast hosting platform that is truly for the podcaster
SecondLine Themes	Custom WordPress themes designed for podcasters

Creative & Strategic Guides

Included in *Altered Audio* and available for adaptation:

- Show Format Blueprint
- Brand Voice Checklist
- Podcast Press Kit Script
- Creator's Manifesto Printout
- Signal Sync Checklist
- Mentorship Outreach Email Script
- Collaboration Request One-Pager
- Partnership & Interview Request

Show Format Blueprint

Outline your podcast's structural rhythm and creative DNA

Podcast Name: ________________________________

Tagline or Elevator Pitch: ____________________

Format Type (circle one):

◯ Solo ◯ Interview ◯ Panel ◯ Narrative ◯ Hybrid

Episode Length Target: ______ **mins**

Cadence: ◯ Weekly ◯ Bi-weekly ◯ Monthly ◯ Seasonal

Segment Breakdown:

1. Intro:

____

2. Main Content:

____

3. Recurring Features:

____

4. Outro / Call-to-Action:

____

Tone & Style:

- ◯ Conversational
- ◯ Informative
- ◯ Story-driven
- ◯ Satirical
- ◯ Inspiring

Music & Sound Design Notes:

____

Guest Criteria (if applicable):

____

Content Pillars or Categories:

- ____
- ____
- ____

Editorial Notes:

Brand Voice Checklist

Define your podcast's personality and values

Your Podcast's Core Voice Traits (choose 3–5):

- ◯ Warm
- ◯ Bold
- ◯ Geeky
- ◯ Witty
- ◯ Reflective
- ◯ Authoritative
- ◯ Playful
- ◯ Empathetic

Is your language more:

- ◯ Casual and conversational
- ◯ Professional and polished
- ◯ Scripted and narrative
- ◯ Spontaneous and raw

Define your mission in one sentence:

___

Three phrases listeners should associate with your brand:

1. ___
2. ___
3. ___

Do you use sound effects or music as part of your brand tone?

◯ Yes ◯ No ◯ Occasionally

Visual Identity Notes (colors, fonts, logos):

___

___

___

___

___

___

Podcast Press Kit Script

Package your podcast for media, guests, and outreach.

Use this when reaching out to media, guests, or collaborators. Keep it concise, visual, and value-driven.

Podcast Name: ______________________________

Logo: [Insert Image or Link] Tagline:

____

Creator(s): __________________________________

Contact: ____________________________________

Website: ____________________________________

Social Links:

Instagram: ________________________

Twitter/X: _________________________

LinkedIn: _________________________

YouTube: _________________________

Patreon/Other: ____________________

Show Description: [1–3 sentences max. What makes your show unique, valuable, and story-driven?]

Notable Guests (if applicable):

____

____

____

Key Topics Covered:

____

____

____

Audience Metrics / Milestones: (Optional)

Total Downloads: _____________________

Episode Frequency: ____________________

Notable Features or Awards: _____________

Availability: ◉ *Guest Interviews* ◉ *Speaking Engagements* ◉ *Sponsorship* ◉ *Cross-Promotion*

Creator's Manifesto Printout

Your creative values, loud and proud

Unleash the Geek in You™ — A Rally Cry for the Passionate and Persistent

- ✅ Create with Purpose
- ✅ Honor the Process
- ✅ Value Every Listener
- ✅ Speak What Matters
- ✅ Stay Curious
- ✅ Lead with Kindness
- ✅ Protect Your Joy
- ✅ Mentor the Next Wave
- ✅ Think Long Game
- ✅ Be Loud. Be Geeky. Be You.

[Signature space]

____

Date: ________________________

☑ Signal Sync Checklist

Tactical guide to activate your creative journey

✅ **Define your show's creative identity (Ch. 1–3)**

✅ **Build a format using the Blueprint above (Ch. 4)**

✅ **Choose 2 monetization models to pilot (Ch. 7)**

✅ **Set your cadence and backup workflows (Ch. 9)**

✅ **Reflect on your purpose before checking metrics (Ch. 12)**

✅ **Draft a podcast press kit**

✅ **Bookmark mentorship tools (Ch. 11)**

✅ **Choose your website platform (Ch. 8–9)**

✅ **Review your brand tone (Brand Voice Checklist)**

✅ **Schedule monthly strategy reviews**

✅ **Print and sign your Creator's Manifesto**

Mentorship Outreach Email Script

Make meaningful connections with emerging creators

Subject: Want to Connect on Podcasting & Creative Growth

Hi [Name],

I'm reaching out after catching your [project/podcast/post], and I really appreciate what you're building. As someone who's been in the podcast space for a while, I've found real value in connecting and supporting newer voices.

If you're open to it, I'd love to offer some mentorship, share insights, and help however I can—whether it's workflow questions, guest outreach tips, or building episode consistency.

Let me know what would be most helpful—I'm here to listen and support.

Thanks again for what you're creating!

Best,

[Your Name]

[Your Podcast / Site]

[Contact Info]

Collaboration Request One-Pager

Pitch tool for guests, partnerships, or co-productions

Podcast Name: ______________________________

Contact Person: ____________________________

Email: ____________________________________

Website / Press Kit: _________________________

Project Type: ◉ *Interview* ◉ *Guest Co-Host* ◉ *Workshop* ◉ *Co-Branded Series*

Collab Topic or Focus: _______________________

What We Bring:

- *A loyal audience of [X] podcast listeners*
- *Cross-promotion via [platforms]*
- *Audio and visual production support*
- *Shared branding assets if applicable*

Our Ideal Partner:

- *Values-aligned creators and organizations*
- *Someone with passion and perspective*
- *Comfortable sharing their expertise or story*

This type of script will help you in the efforts of contacting and reaching out to an organization to gauge interest for collaboration.

Partnership & Interview Request

Adaptable for Actor Interviews, Product Reviews, and Sponsorship Outreach

Obviously, this will be tailored to the person/organization but this gives you a general idea of what you *could* send to get some attention.

> *Subject: Collaboration Opportunity with [website]*
>
> *Hi [Name or Brand Team],*
>
> *Hope you're doing well! I'm reaching out from [website], a podcast dedicated to [subject matter]—from storytelling and interviews to product reviews and fan-driven commentary.*
>
> *Whether it's showcasing your latest products, sharing your story, or co-creating something exciting—our goal is to spotlight people and projects that move the geek culture forward.*
>
> *We offer:*
>
> 🎙️ *In-depth podcast interviews and product spotlights*
>
> 📺 *Dynamic video features to bring your brand to life*
>
> 📸 *Written reviews and editorial coverage for our website and social platforms*
>
> *If you're open to exploring a collaboration or interview feature, we'd love to chat and find the best fit. Let us know what works for you, and we'll make it easy.*

This type of script will help you in the efforts of contacting and reaching out to an organization to gauge interest for interview and outreach.

About the Author

🎙️ ALTERED AUDIO Podcasting Demystified — Clear Advice, Real Tools, and Zero Gatekeeping

Steve "Megatron" Phillips didn't set out to be a podcaster. Armed with a $9 mic and a dream of voice acting, he stumbled into fan dubs, fell headfirst into geek culture, and helped shape one of the longest-running independent podcast networks online.

Now, with over 20 years of hard-earned experience behind the mic, Phillips is pulling back the curtain. *Altered Audio* is a story-rich, approachable guide for creators who crave clarity—not gatekeeping. Forget jargon and perfectionism—this book gives you practical tools, geek wisdom, and a healthy dose of inspiration to help launch your voice into the world.

Whether you're a pop culture junkie, total beginner, or someone rediscovering your creative spark, *Altered Audio* is your backstage pass to building a podcast that truly matters.

No ego. No fluff. Just real talk from someone who's lived it.

www.ingramcontent.com/pod-product-compliance
Lightning Source LLC
LaVergne TN
LVHW022057200926
848481LV00003B/953